We Can Count 123

Written by Karen O'Callaghan

Illustrated by Linda Worrall
and Steve Ling

Cover design by Oxprint Ltd

Edited by Debbie Lines

ISBN 0 86112 579 7
Published by Brimax Books, Newmarket, England 1990.
Second printing 1990.
Printed in Spain by Graficromo S.A., Cordoba.

We can count

Brimax Books · Newmarket · England

We Can Count 123

These pages are designed to encourage children to observe and count objects within their own environment.

Counting Our Toys from 1–10 is the basic section. Each page shows the number as a symbol, a numeral and a written word – three ways to explain simply to a child the number concept. Colours are also introduced.

Counting at Home/Outside/In the Supermarket – These are familiar situations for children everywhere which stimulate their interest. The child is invited to join in, to find and count using the illustrated number/picture/word key. Repetition of this concept can be used by parents to help children count the numerous objects they can see around them.

The ideas are expanded further to include the order and grouping of numbers, counting backwards, and to show the various activities and games your child can follow.

All children love rhymes. The number rhymes provide a fun way to establish solid and basic number concepts.

Given the examples in these pages, parents can develop new games with their children which involve numbers and counting.

Learning numbers can be great fun.

Alex and Zoe
are counting their toys.
Turn the pages and you can count too.

one rocking horse

| • | 1 | **one** |

two bicycles

| •• | 2 | **two** |

three boats

| ••• | 3 | **three** |

four teddy bears

| :: | 4 | **four** |

five dolls

| :•: | 5 | **five** |

six balls

| :::: | 6 | **six** |

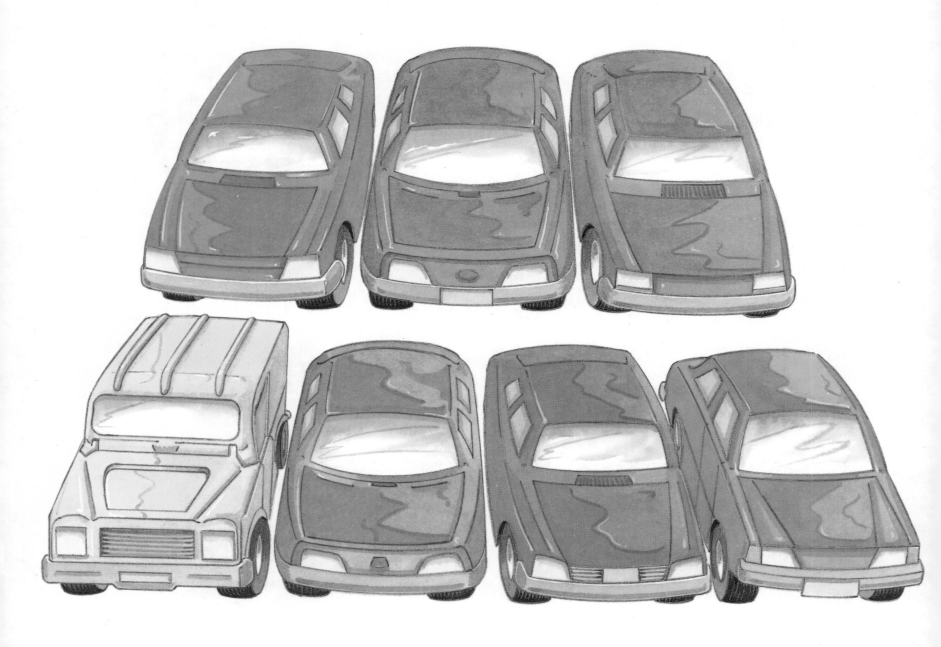

seven cars

| ∴∴ • | 7 | **seven** |

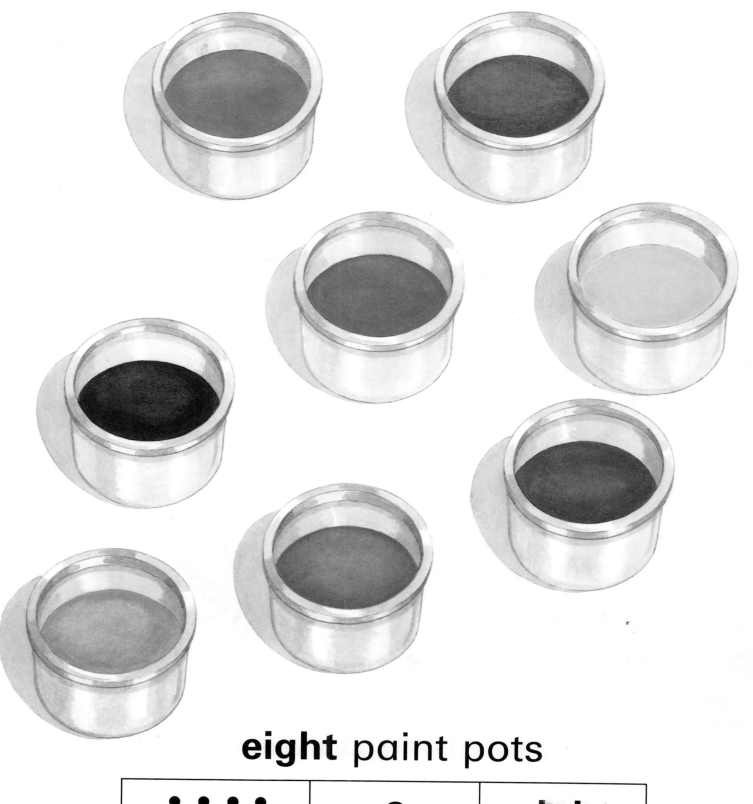

eight paint pots

| :::: :::: | 8 | **eight** |

nine farm animals

| ::::: • | 9 | **nine** |

ten balloons

| ⣿ | 10 | **ten** |

Alex and Zoe are having a party.
Can you find . . .?

1	cake
2	jugs
3	bowls
4	glasses
5	spoons
6	candles
7	plates
8	straws
9	buns
10	cookies

Counting outside
Can you find . . .?

1		church
2		buses
3		trucks
4		bicycles
5		cars
6		street lights
7		birds
8		houses
9		trees
10		people

Counting in the supermarket
Find and count with us . . .

1		chicken
2		loaves
3		cartons of milk
4		packets of butter
5		cans of beans
6		eggs
7		yoghurts
8		oranges
9		tomatoes
10		burgers

We can make a number stairway with bricks. Can you?

Count with us to the top
and back down again.

Counting backwards

"Help me with the countdown," says Zoe. "Are you ready?"

6

7

8

9

10

"We have lift off!" says Alex.
"We are off to the moon."

0

1

2

3

4

Let's make a long train.

1st   2nd   3rd   4th   5th

"I am first, I am the driver," says Zoe.

6th   7th   8th   9th   10th

"I am last, I am the guard," says Alex.

We are sorting our toys.
We can put our bricks

in 5's

in 2's

in 4's

in 3's

Alex has sorted the toys into . . .

2		blue
3		green
4		yellow
5		red

Zoe has put together . . .

2		planes
3		cars
4		boats
5		balls

Join in our counting rhyme

There were **10** in the bed . . .
And the little one said,
"Roll over, roll over!"
So they all rolled over
And one fell out.

There were **9** in the bed . . .
And the little one said,
"Roll over, roll over!"
So they all rolled over
And one fell out.

There were **8** in the bed . . .
And the little one said,
"Roll over, roll over!"
So they all rolled over
And one fell out.

There were **7** in the bed . . .
And the little one said,
"Roll over, roll over!"
So they all rolled over
And one fell out.

There were **6** in the bed . . .
And the little one said,
"Roll over, roll over!"
So they all rolled over
And one fell out.

There were **5** in the bed . . .
And the little one said,
"Roll over, roll over!"
So they all rolled over
And one fell out.

There were **4** in the bed . . .
And the little one said,
"Roll over, roll over!"
So they all rolled over
And one fell out.

There were **3** in the bed . . .
And the little one said,
"Roll over, roll over!"
So they all rolled over
And one fell out.

There were **2** in the bed . . .
And the little one said,
"Roll over, roll over!"
So they both rolled over
And one fell out.

There was **1** in the bed . . .
And the little one said,
"Roll over, roll over!"
So she rolled over
And she fell out.

There were none in the bed
And no one said,
"Roll over, roll over!"
"We are all down here!"
How many on the floor?

Say this counting rhyme with us

One red engine puffing down the track
One red engine puffing puffing back.

Two blue engines puffing down the tra
Two blue engines puffing puffing back.

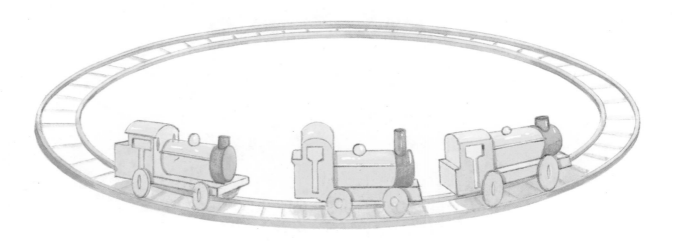

Three yellow engines puffing down the track
Three yellow engines puffing puffing back.

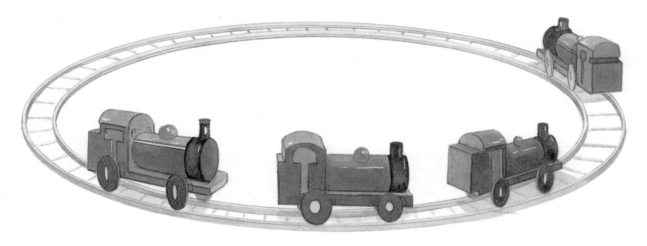

Four green engines puffing down the track
Four green engines puffing puffing back.

Five orange engines puffing down the track
Five orange engines puffing puffing back.